MORALS OF A FREE MARKET

INTEREST AND IT'S SPECIAL INTERESTS
THE ROOT CAUSE FOR ALL SOCIAL-ECONOMIC PROBLEMS

FIRST REVISION – TO BE CONTINUED

By

FLORIAN T. WOS

MORALS OF A FREE MARKET

INTEREST AND IT'S SPECIAL INTERESTS

THE ROOT CAUSE FOR ALL SOCIAL-ECONOMIC PROBLEMS

FIRST REVISION – TO BE CONTINUED

By

FLORIAN F. WOS

First Draft Published, August 15, 2014

ISBN-13: 978-1508821168

Dedicated to my father.

With the hope to achieve human dignity for everyone.

CONTENTS

PREFACE

This book should not be considered as a big-headed guideline or ready to be applied solution in the current critical state of our democratic capitalism. And – due to my German origin – there are without doubt more scientific or better written books about this broad topic. Instead, I hope that some of my over the years collected ideas and personal opinions about our interest driven financial system provide ground for discussion to the select few that might be interested in my writings. As this book is written without any scientific or analytical references, any untitled notes, quotations or intentional empty spaces are solely for esthetic reasons.

ACKNOWLEDGMENTS

I'm grateful for every day I feel the sense of hope to pursue. I'm grateful to everyone who kept me in his thoughts, even though the circumstances and odds that piled up against me since 1992 guided me onto a path that happened to result in this book. I'm thankful to myself for my ability to stay calm and keep my temper despite my very unique personal situation in the previous years. As much I am thankful for my ability to disassociate from these other threatening topics from time to time.

As the remaining part of this life came more than once so close to never happen, I also thank god for guiding me since the very day.

9

PART I

MORALS OF A FREE MARKET

INTRODUCTION

Over the course of this short book, I'd like to express some of my personal opinions about our interest driven economical system but also solutions I gathered over the years. Applied, they could eradicate almost all negative impact our current capitalistic free market economy has to our society, but in a way that would not restrict innovation and individual freedoms as seen in socialistic systems.

A world where the middle class does well,
but everyone else too.

A world where the middle class does well, but everyone else too.

"*A system, providing equal legal and labor rights, equal access to education, health and elderly-care as fundamental human rights no matter of financial heritage or class.*"

"*A system, with a smart and unified taxation model, eradicating approximately 90% of the administrative overhead while providing a healthier nutrition to it's citizens.*"

"*A system, with rules that limit the influence of corporate interests, with restrictions that are economically, socially and environmentally friendly*"

BETWEEN CAPITALISM AND WAR

In the early 20th century, people had the faith it will always go forward to a more civilized and educated society. The majority of the population were able to read and write, and also morally everything pointed in a direction to be optimistic.

Until the first world war initiated an era of tragedy that ended up killing more people than ever during the whole century.

On the materialistic side, the world improved for almost everyone, but ideologically and morally we were unable to catch up with the advancements of our modern industrial age that for the first time allowed for the killing of so many people. It rather happened to be a progress in the reverse direction, leaving – after it all settled – our modern form of capitalism that even until today is the cause for disasters on a regular basis. Exploiting everything and everyone, from the environment to our health, from our family's well being to our moral ethics, increasingly cutting the branch our modern society relies on so much; Human dignity.

*On the materialistic side,
the world improved for
almost everyone..*

Yet during the last half of the century, any rational analysis of our current form of capitalism had been systematically denied due to it's obvious and many advantages compared to it's previous unsuccessful alternatives. Unrelated from the best intent they might have had from a moral aspect, and unrelated from the competition with other capitalistic economies that lead to their downfall.

But our faith that a less regulated market will fix everything by itself kept us from taking note of this ever increasing crisis that once again built up so unnoticed during the last decade.

The current ongoing and still developing crisis reached a completely new quality, likely surpassing the great depression of the 30's that once ended in the second world war.

And today – not only considering the outcome of another world war – it is even more dramatic and no-one seems to have a solution for the current situation as it never existed before. The very situation created be the faith in our neo-liberal financial system, at a time when previous crisis already exposed so many downsides of it.

Right now, at a time when the major worlds economies still seem to rely on each other, recent developments appear to be the first signs that not only the competition for the world's resources is already getting tougher, but also the underlying monetary system itself appears to reach it's limits at the same time. With the only forecast of a downward spiral, until every last resource is fully developed and the first actual shortages end up in ever increasing conflicts between national economical interests.

...

The current situation of continuously increasing geopolitical tensions – to a large extend related to the worldwide economical situation and fight for remaining gas- and oil reserves – could be a first example to that.

"The first panacea for a mismanaged nation is inflation of the currency; the second is war. Both bring a temporary prosperity; both bring a permanent ruin. But both are the refuge of political and economic opportunists."

– Ernest Hemingway

3

OUR 'FREEDOM' CALLED FREE MARKET ECONOMY

Our current – 'freedom' called – free market economy works in theory and if everyone applies to the same set of moral ethics. But in reality, everyone and every company is looking for its own calculable advantage according to the very lax rules of the game. An obvious fact, that is in-debatable not only from an objective point of view.

Therefore, our current form of free market capitalism isn't much different from simple anarchy for those with enough criminal and financial power to defeat it's few regulations. An open playground for special interests, with almost no actual boundaries as long as legal fees are a calculable part of the business model. A mostly unregulated playground for large corporations without almost no actual risks to be held accountable for the destruction of the environment or health of the population.

But even with the repeating history of collapses, what already had been understood about these negative sides of capitalism had simply been forgotten over all the prosperous decades. There just had never been enough reason to criticize it's downsides with all the innovation it made possible. Not even when the many negative consequences for the environment and our health became more obvious in the recent decades.

Side effects of our neo-liberal economy; From the well known problems such as carbon emissions and climate change, deforestation and pollution of our oceans to additives and pesticides in our nutrition. Collateral side effects that many would account to our modern industrialization itself and not the economical system, but it's in fact the undermining of existing restrictions by corporate interest and criminal energy – both result of a mostly unregulated and ruthless market – that only further increases most of these unnecessary problems.

"Capital as such is not evil; it is its wrong use that is evil. Capital in some form or other will always be needed."

– Mahatma Gandhi

4

A SYSTEM THAT PREVENTS GREED BY DESIGN

Man – without rules – will always be greedy. What's needed is a system that prevents greed and financial influence by corporate interests and special interest groups by design. Comparable to the democratic capitalism we consider as our current political system, but with fair rules and the exact same rights and opportunities, independent from financial heritage or class.

A system that simply declares the most irresponsible financial products or profits solely based on compound interest as illegal. A system that guarantees the exact same legal rights and access to education, health and elderly-care mandatory for everyone, and with a smart taxation model that assures that everyone gives the exact same percent of his fair share. But obviously a fair share taken additional to a very bottom life-standard to be equally fair for everyone.

From the student or minimum wage worker to the highest income; taxation and healthcare should always be a fixed percentage taken from above the average minimum cost of living to guarantee equal opportunities. Likewise, no-one should be able to profit from the returns of interest alone without generating any additional value to a society, while everyone else struggles to pay for the interest or even compound interest.

Economies that allow for greed of any kind might always have an advantage in competition with other economical systems, but will never be able to sustain themselves over a long period of time. And as of now, were most of the worlds economies are heading right for next collapse, there are even less reasons to hold onto beliefs that already failed in the past only because alternative political belief systems had failed too.

In either way, capitalism – on it's own – will always be unstable by design, if the interest driven financial system allows for the accumulation of financial influence to stretch even the most fundamental rules. An economy that allows for the unlimited accumulation of wealth, with interest and compound interest, debt and compound debt that is progressing exponentially is always inevitably heading for collapses or crises of varying duration. Not only out of selfish or irrational human behavior alone, but as a mathematical consequence of the underlying economical and monetary system itself.

And even with unlimited shades between black and white, capitalism, socialism, communism and other political belief systems with the same ending; Human rights and fair rules should apply to every political mindset, including the ones that failed in the past. But no matter how deeply indoctrinated in the minds of a population, the current form of capitalism we sustain – at least in it's sole form – will disappear sooner or later in either way.

What we especially need is to stop this self-refuting ideology of maximum and unlimited growth by any means, and the naive mindset an unregulated market could ever govern itself. A free market – driven by a financial system that allows for the unlimited accumulation of interest – can and will never be moral and free of greed as interest itself had never been moral. Not only in the scriptures of pretty much all religions, but from a common sense perspective too.

Instead, investment into innovation by an increasingly number of smaller sized businesses should not only be the gold standard from a moral aspect, but just mandatory. Investment into businesses as the only option for wealth to be accumulated, opposed to an infinite accumulation of wealth as an increasingly digital currency alone.

Therefore, currency – that obviously resembles the value of lifetime and workforce in exchange for goods and services – should always be in the system to fulfill it's role as a medium of trade. And not much more.

Imposing higher environmental standards could be a first smart option to stimulate the economy at times when other stimulus already failed, but the current state of lobby influence pretty much prevents any such novel approach from ever happen. Moreover, even with so many prosperous years, we simply can not return to the same form of top-to-bottom capitalism of the recent century, as much as future can never be a continuation of the past.

The solution lies in the right combination of fair rules for everyone, but making sure that the moral ethics we already agree on as a society are actually in effect and binding.

Obviously, that leads to greater governmental influence and restrictions to some extend, but in a way that would prevent any unfair exploitation by lobbying and special interests. And of course in a way that our individual or privacy rights are not violated by larger semi-private corporations either. Rules and restrictions that already passed legislation decades ago, with an additional new set of rules for the revenue required to further enforce them.

A unified taxation model – as detailed in the later chapters – that subjects as much positive and negative aspects of our daily life's as possible to either taxation or subsidize could be a first solution to that.

"The first truth is that the liberty of a democracy is not safe if the people tolerate the growth of private power to a point where it becomes stronger than their democratic State itself. That, in its essence, is fascism — ownership of government by an individual, by a group or by any other controlling private power."

– Franklin D. Roosevelt

Suddenly, September 15, 2008, the day of the collapse of Lehman Brothers exposed for the first time in history the fundamental flaw of an unregulated market to a broader public.

Unrestrained greed, that almost gambled away not only the financial foundations of many citizens but also the moral foundations of our society. And not only turned the housing market crisis that had a big part in it worldwide when millions already lost their homes and jobs as a result of it, but most of the world governments even united to bail-out the ones responsible for it when the whole global financial system threatened to collapse after all.

But until today, where the accumulated public debt is now endangering everything once again, politicians in charge are still unable to admit that not the individual 'bad banks' but their failed policies related to the financial system itself are the actual root cause that lead to all these problems. From the many questionable financial products sold by mortgage bankers to unaware seniors to the gamble with the well known 'credit default swaps' that only further added to the existing mortgage crisis.

And it's still the exact same fraction – the one once responsible for the unregulated market and it's previous crisis – that is expecting the taxpayer – in fact mostly the bottom half of taxpayers – to pay for it all, believing that after another short period of governmental intervention everything will be as it was before. Ready for the next gamble, while everything else fell apart already.

"Faites vos jeux. Rien ne va plus!"

Wealth that accumulated in the shares of large corporations is sometimes diminished by hysteria of the stock market alone. Wisdom and documentations archived by generations have to be completely redone, only due to the quick merger of two equities. Office floors left empty, almost brand new machines dumped in the trashcan. Patents are kept on hold due to court decisions and frozen assets. Daily hysteria of the market and high frequency trading diminish achievements of generations by a mouse-click on a daily basis, but completely unnoticed by the broader public.

And today, almost like our digital lifestyle is already exploited by advertising companies and a few large monopoly's of software, also the moral aspect of our political foundation turned out to be so much cracked from the inside with the latest worldwide surveillance revealings. Unforeseen revealings of a mostly corporate interest governed, semi-private surveillance infrastructure used for the analysis of consumer behavior in the same way as industrial espionage for governmental interests. Tracking of users across multiple devices, from the office PC's to the tablets, smartphones, smart televisions and gaming consoles. A perfect example for exploitation of every aspects of life in the age of our neo-liberal economy.

Almost as unforeseen – but at a time where we need it the most – there appears to be not a single equivalent political system able to provide for everyone but the upper half of us. And with the major belief systems that only allow for a decision between capitalism and socialism – or in other words a decision between wrong and worse – nobody seems to have a solution to get out of the crisis, because the situation we have today never existed before in the same outreach.

...

"We are in danger of destroying ourselves by our greed and stupidity. We cannot remain looking inwards at ourselves on a small and increasingly polluted and overcrowded planet."

– *Stephen* Hawking

5

CURRENCY & LIFETIME

Obviously, every amount of work that is done in a society equals the amount of lifetime of each individual performing the task, while at the same time, our current interest driven economy will always allow for the accumulation of this lifetime to the benefit of a select few. A system very efficiently squeezing the most amount of work out of everyone, but without everyone benefiting from it in the same way.

An equation that might easily be compared to the decades of work involved in the building of large monuments in our early history. In the end, there happened to be this large pyramid or statue that involved the life's work of hundreds of thousands of workers, with many unsurpassed human accomplishments we are still astonished about today. But how many cultural advancements can be directly related to the building process itself? And how much other goals could have been achieved during the same time with the same amount of workforce in an educated society we have today? Apart from the vision their gifted architects had once intended with it, what remains today are at least monuments of historic value.

Unlike our today's architectural super-projects, who usually provide to a greater benefit of faster transit or urban infrastructure for later generations, our current form of top to bottom capitalism – even though with many of the same ancient similarities – will more likely leave a disaster of historic proportion than a world wonder.

Still, capitalism in itself is unquestioned due to all the positive effects a highly competitive and often ruthless market seems to provide to a majority of us. Overseen is the administrative overhead or work that could have been automated decades ago, but is hold onto because all the lobby influence simply does not allow for smart regulations or drastic changes in the public sector. Overseen are all the negative effects of ever increasing monopoly's of power that dictate every aspect of our life's, from the software we rely on to the sugary beverages we drink.

And much of our accumulated wealth today is even spent for personal agendas that are contra-productive to a greater good, over-idealistic or simply consume the workforce for the luxury of a few individuals.

Luxury, that, by times is more just the prestige of something, than actual an enhanced quality of life. A golden watch – assuming made of real gold – is from an objective point of view just about two times as heavy on the wrist than an of-the-shelf model, but still there is a demand for it. A psychology behind prestige that's hard to understand from an average income perspective.

In contrary, sometimes we don't even value the amount of work involved in our average day-to-day goods. Every cheap handwoven shirt we might throw away due to a small imperfection –

at the same time – also equals lifetime of an industrial worker in a developing country who under different circumstances might have become the greatest artist or inventor of modern times. With the potential providing for everyone at a later point in life, but turned into a lost possibility; preselected by the place of birth, preselected by heritage.

In that respect and with the private side of our own educational system in mind, an inefficiency and unbalance by the selection of talent between social classes we should not be able to afford.

...

"Child labor and poverty are inevitably bound together and if you continue to use the labor of children as the treatment for the social disease of poverty, you will have both poverty and child labor to the end of time."

– Grace Abbott

INTRINSIC MOTIVATION

What is unknown is how many scientific breakthroughs could be achieved by a so called 'intrinsic motivation' alone if a society is increasingly set free of self-reasoned financial bureaucracy and large monopoly's. Leaving more time to rest in a population and space for new ideas. Especially for the younger generation that today receives the most amount of pressure at an age were social-cultural aspects of life are at least as much important as fields of science. Assuming that surge for solutions to daily social- or health related problems would be a common mindset that is taught in schools, with a minimum amount of hurdles for the implementation of smarter regulations that provide to a greater benefit even large idealistic projects that were once unthinkable could be taken on. Assumed if guided by common sense.

However, what's mostly thought in schools is how to become an efficient narrow minded specialist in an obedient population of workers. Smart enough for the task the industry demands in one of it's many niche sectors – no matter how technological advanced today – but less capable of critical thinking or even questioning anything between all the interesting gossip and entertainment on television. Less capable to reflect about all the bad aspects of the world we live in – from environmental or social issues to unhealthy nutrition – unable to voice an opinion because what is defined as common sense is already and unquestionable dictated by an elite circle of corporate media networks and publishers. The same – mostly advertising and special interest financed – large news outlets and monopolies that are conceived to educate the population, but are under close inspection only a representation of corporate interests. With a few good exceptions of course.

7

THE ALMOST INEVITABLE COLLAPSE

At the moment, it's becoming more obvious that we're heading for an implosion rather then just a collapse of the financial system. The Ponzi-Scheme of corporate capitalism that always continues to work as long as it's broad base of debt feeds more money into it has just reached it's 70 year life-cycle once more again. And now, where the accumulation of debt and interest outgrowths even the smartest last ditch approaches, the crash is almost inevitable. If not predictable just according to the given situation.

And the policies that lead us to all this are quite obvious too. Instead of programs and standards focused on new innovation or increased manufacturing and export, the common approach by most of the world governments used to be pretty much only the generation of money. Either just printed or created by loans and low interest, without generating any actual value. The naive approach of exponential growth only by monetary policy alone; a paradox in itself.

But perhaps the top-to-bottom form of capitalism we have now can only end up in such a giant disaster, as those in charge and benefiting from it right now would never let go of it on their own. Only uncertain is, how we are going to react when our all lifestyles we cherish so much abruptly end due to a devastating devaluation of our currencies when the Ponzi-Scheme just collapses again. And even worse; – considering the irrational human behavior at previous shortages – how are we going to react when we realize that the ones responsible in fact imposed it that way? With a broad range of outcomes, from Inflation to even hyperinflation depending on further attempts to fix the market, it's even harder to predict the next months. But the first precursors to a giant collapse appear to slowly take effect already.

And even with all the billions previously flushed into the economy as a stimulus to keep the mathematical illusion going, the ones in charge right now simply don't know what else to do. Instead, they rather try to wage war at a time were the battle for the remaining world resources, agriculture, water and energy had already begun. Greed, that never used to care about environmental restrictions before – taking part in destroying not only the ecological system for the maximum amount of profit – now even continues to jeopardize the monetary system itself at a time were we are heading for a disaster already. And the gamble still continues.

But a solution for all these current problems is impossible without a fundamental change of our beliefs, not only by a few new rules we agree on.

In the remaining chapters of this short book, I'd like to express some of my over the years collected ideas that I think are necessary in the long-term for a sustainable society, that at the same time also guarantees individual freedoms and allows for the success of individuals.

...

"There is a sufficiency in the world for man's need but not for man's greed."

– Mahatma Gandhi

PART II

EFFICIENCY & STANDARDS

8

THE EFFICIENCY OF OUR FINANCIAL SYSTEM

The current form of capitalism we sustain has one advantage that makes it so efficient in competition with any other economical systems as it guarantees that every possible bit of innovation is squeezed out of a struggling and hard working population.

Only overseen are the negative effects that an ever increasing accumulation of financial influence and special interests has to our daily life's. From the overall quality of our nutrition, weakened each day by undermining even the bare minimum amount of common sense health standards to the longevity of consumer goods that are intentionally manufactured to break after a certain time.

And even with all the positive effects of a highly competitive market that removes the worst or most inefficient products or services thanks to the competition itself, there is still an increasingly larger number of niches dictated by only a few known brands each day. The same major brands we all know; the ones with larger scandals by time. But still mostly unknown how very few major conglomerates there are actually behind all these brands. Increasingly less forced to care about their customers. Less interested in the efficiency or health impact of their products in the long-term. By times, not even motivated to invest into innovation at all, as long as sales of the established products continue, especially in the food sector.

The same traditional, mostly sugar and trans-fat laden food items manufactured to the same recipes of the last century, even though new nutritional revealings exposed them as the main cause for many diseases. And even though awareness about many of these unhealthy products became common sense already, expensive advertising campaigns and new packaging design still continues to keep them in the supermarket shelf's.

Having in mind that many scientific niches today require almost more than a whole life's work to become firm the field of research, the quality of our nutrition and therefore longevity and health of a population could actually be one of the most important factors for innovation in the future.

Another two major sides of an efficiency of capitalism that counteract each other. On the one side, the free market economy, highly efficient in yielding innovation by a ruthless competition, on the other side efficiently leading to health- and environmental related problems and a shorter lifespan.

A not negligible inefficiency in regards to scientific breakthroughs that are often honored as lifetime achievements, with an unknown estimate how many potential breakthroughs are lost just due to a slightly lower life expectancy.

9

INTEREST AS A CAUSE FOR INFLATION

Interest – throughout history – has always been criticized and ethically questioned by pretty much all religions, but also by many economists of our modern time. Contrary to all moral ethics, but still a universal law that automatically applies to every civilization with the need to trade goods.

Whenever there is any form of currency in a society, there is always the possibility for someone to lent his savings for the profit of interest.

But pretty much unnoticed is the inflating effect of interest itself. Any monetary system that allows for interest always leads to a latent inflation due to the increasing amount of currency generated out of thin air by every single loan taking place.

A bank might lent 100.000, but writes the projected 125.000 in it's books. Mathematically a 25 percent inflation because the additional 25.000 are created out of liability alone, yet unnoticed due to the deflating effect by the accumulation of wealth that takes place at the same time. The bank has now – on paper –

25.000 more that need to be generated in a competing market by the loan taker, even though the 25.000 have already been created the very second the loan was signed on paper and all potential losses already been calculated.

Mathematically, an inflation according to the total amount of currency in the system, but a deflating effect in the competing market niche that needs to generate the additional amount of interest or even compound interest of it. Another paradox and inefficiency of interest – in regards to use of lifetime in a society – that is easier to understand by plain math then from an economical background.

...

"Compound interest is the eighth wonder of the world. He who understands it, earns it ... he who doesn't ... pays it."

– Albert Einstein

10

ERADICATING LOBBY-ISM
AT IT'S SOURCE

There are enough books about the ethics and morality of professional lobbying I'd be able to go into much detail about this broad topic, but the long term impact – especially to our all health – is in my opinion so drastic that any form of lobbying should simply be declared illegal. As simple as that.

No matter of industry or niche, any form of corporate lobbying our finance oblique political system provides ground to will always negatively influence either the environment, our health or the quality of our all life's to some extend. Not only considering long-term effects to our health when common sense restrictions are only slightly undermined by the tiniest amount, but especially in the case of larger food scandals with products that turned out to contain questionable or undeclared carcinogenic additives.

In either way, there is simply not a single positive reason for the legality of lobby-ism, neither in the financial-, food-, agriculture, consumer-, or pharmaceutical industry that could ever outweigh the negative effects of it.

And not only because the word 'lobby-ism' already implies a profit driven interest in itself, but also because the imposing of common sense restrictions is already paid for by the taxpayer. And obviously not with the intent to be weakened by corporate interests the other day.

Somehow comparable to a community that collects for a good cause, not to realize later on that all efforts diminished just out of selfish interests by a few. Something that obviously would never be tolerated if happening so blatantly, but behind the curtains of political sponsoring and legislation it happens everyday.

...

11

A SOCIETIES MOST INFLUENTIAL FACTORS

From an analytical point of view, the first and foremost influential factor to our society is our all health, and therefore the quality of our environment and our nutrition.

In that respect, it should be only common sense that the industry that supplies our food but also the pharmaceutical industry in a broader sense – unlike less impacting consumer goods – has to be free from any form of lobbying by law.

But the reality shows that it is in fact the food and the pharmaceutical industry that are exposed to the most amount of corporate interests and lobby influence. And obviously, these special interests will usually not lead to less polluted food products at the same price or drugs that are thoroughly tested with the best intentions, but rather products that are either of less quality – by times even without any nutritional value at all – or even with unpredictable long-term effects.

But almost as important is of course also the environmental impact to our nutrition. From the many unforeseen long-term effects of small traces of industrial pollution, questionable pesticides or accumulating by-products of industrial fertilizers. No matter how small the amount, once allowed to end up in the environment it will always end up in our systems in the same way and accumulate over time. The well known glyphosate, a common herbicide especially used in GMO agriculture could be a good example after recent study confirmed high levels of the chemical in 70 percent of households drinking water and even in in 3 out of 10 samples of breast milk taken. Another perfect example of a recent scandal that disappeared from the mainstream media within just a few days.

The later detailed unified taxation model that not only generates additional revenue, but counterweights many such negative influences directly could be a first approach for a solution to this problem.

12

PATENTS & INNOVATION

Patents will always be a double edged sword. On the one side, they guarantee the inventor's intellectual property rights but they can also be a burden for innovation the more intellectual property accumulates in the portfolios of large corporations, especially in the case of software patents and key technologies.

A smart patent system should guarantee that after a certain amount of financial success, technologies become publicly available to be re-used without costly licensing. Or in the case of completely unused patents, after a certain amount of time. Another significant point is that in our solely profit-driven market, new ideas are mostly not even based on 'what's good', but rather based on who is in the position to dictate them into the market niche, with only a few rare exceptions of an evolutionary benefit to our society. An example could be the paradigm shift the iPhone and later iPad brought up – criticized as almost dictated against the market in the beginning, but then increasingly accepted and redefining the whole category later on.

In contrast, often even the most idealistic ideas fail due to the harsh reality of actual consumer demands, with a late near bankruptcy of an electric-car manufacturer as one example. In that respect, a patent system that is even more equally fair for smaller start-up should be common sense.

In terms of the intellectual property rights of individuals, there should be drastic sanctions in cases of individuals or former employers being defrauded of their rightful share on patents or developments by larger corporations. Not only from an ethical perspective, but to prevent misuse of the additional gained economical influence without granting the individual a say in further developments.

A Personal Note: Preferably, the most appropriate form of capital punishment to the most responsible ones involved, executed by the defrauded individual himself.

"Technology is nothing. What's important is that you have a faith in people, that they're basically good and smart, and if you give them tools, they'll do wonderful things with them."

– Steve Jobs

13

ENERGY EFFICIENCY & STANDARDS

While there are enough energy efficiency standards for electrical appliances and electronics already, what is seldom considered is the total amount of energy consumed during the production and transport of products that are used on a daily basis. A more precise taxation system, as detailed in the later chapters could enforce the use of lighter weight materials for travel accessories, from luggage, trolleys to large cargo boxes and transport containers could be a first **example** of that. But also smaller day-to-day items carried around and adding to the energy consumption in public transportation are often overseen.

Taking into account that a usual – up to 6kg heavy – cheaper **business** trolley or hardcase ads approx. 2-3% of weight to each traveler, including 2-3% of weight that is added by over-weight electronics accessories, charging bricks, thick rubber cables and other travel items and accessories, a new weight efficiency standard for travel-related products and luggage could lead to an overall energy use reduction of 1-3% in the public transportation sector alone. Additional to a potential weight reduction by a healthier nutrition, the increasing use of alternative means of **transport** like bicycles as a side effect of a more health and environmental aware society could have an even larger impact on the overall environmental footprint than other restrictions combined.

Generally, **programs** to promote energy awareness beyond home appliances as a guide for a more minimalistic and carbon efficient lifestyle of a society. Additional to tighter restrictions for use of certain materials in specific industries, the existing energy efficiency restriction for energy saving light bulbs and electronics could be further strengthened in regards to even lower energy requirements for LED based lighting, monitors and televisions.

PART III

EQUAL OPPORTUNITIES FOR EVERYONE

14

SERVICES THAT MUST BE PUBLIC ONLY

There are aspects of our life that should be equally available for everyone, no matter of age, social status or financial heritage to guarantee equal fundamental humans rights. Common sense defines these categories as Education, Health and Elderly-care, further detailed in the following chapters. But also a bank account that is free from unnecessary fees and that can't be terminated should be an unquestionable human right.

Considering the also later detailed bank-account based income and revenue taxation model, such a public bank account would also meet two requirements at once. A public identifier for taxation but also a socially guaranteed payment method in our digital age.

Further, from the perspective of the predictable shift from physical currencies to digital only means of payment within just the next few years, such a guaranteed bank account also becomes a fundamental right in the same way there have never been restrictions or even fees for citizens to carry a wallet.

No matter if full or empty.

15

EDUCATIONAL EQUALITY

Any education system should always provide equal opportunities for everyone, independent from financial heritage, class or limited public scholarship programs that preselect on the principle of luck or even sports talent. In regards to access to education as a fundamental human right, all educative facilities should be public only, and not only the elementary and fundamental stages quoted in the 'Universal Declaration of Human Rights, Article 26.i.'

In that respect, it should be common sense that any of the previous quota based funding programs that only allow for a limited number of students have to be phased out and any form of education – from the elementary-, high school to the university stages – declared 'public only' by law.

And despite all the financial interests on the private side, a 'public only' educational system has by no means to be less competitive compared to other countries with mostly private funded systems. In fact, the shift from the requirement of physical presence in classrooms and education material **that** no longer needs to be acquired in physical form, it has become even easier to allow every student the access to the same educational **material** with equally spread fees or subsidies that are shared accordingly between all previous private facilities, public schools or universities.

Equal **opportunities** that ultimately lead to a slightly more efficient election of talent for jobs of future generations, without an unnecessary preselection between different social classes.

...

"It is a miracle that curiosity survives formal education." – Albert Einstein

16

HEALTHCARE EQUALITY

Contrary to the current situation, a public health- and elderly care system that is centered to provide service for everyone according the latest scientific standards. While also making sure that common prescription drugs are equally available for everyone, unrelated from financial status and independent from the financial interests of the pharmaceutical industry to yield the highest returns. Instead of our mostly private funded and increasingly pharmaceutical lobbying influenced healthcare system, a shift towards a more transparent system with treatments that are – by law – equal to everyone as a long-term goal, but at first with revenue generation that is equally fair shared by equally fair healthcare plans. From the human rights perspective of survival, healthcare fees – unlike taxes that are debatable to some extend – should always be a fixed percentage from an individuals income, but taking the minimum cost of living as personal allowance into account.

"It is health that is real wealth and not pieces of gold and silver." – *Mahatma Gandhi*

17

SOCIAL EQUALITY

Not to be mistaken by socialism as much as the title might suggest an equal redistribution of wealth. Instead, to have the same fair opportunities for everyone, what is needed are rules to impose a circulating and debt free currency without infinite accumulation as digital currency on it's own.

An increased taxation of solely interest based profits could be a first option to that. Making it mandatory for wealth to be invested either into new start-ups or shares of corporations, but decreasingly into private equity or modernization of existing real estate that is only slightly generating additional value for a society.

In the same way, educational equality assures fair educational opportunities for everyone, social equality further defines that almost effortless profits in the financial- and the public housing market are limited to a specific amount and do not accumulate infinitely. Especially at a time when drastic changes in the job market continue to increase unemployment rates each day and even larger parts of the society become unable to keep up with the bare minimum cost of living. Another side effect of globalization, when cheap consumer products and imports from developing countries became so convenient for everyone, but the costs of living in our society – largely accounted to private interest rates, housing speculation and food prices – increased simultaneously.

A re-allotment program of public land to applicable citizens – obviously under the highest environmental restrictions – could be an alternative option for a 'de-urbanization' of overly dense populated areas while providing new opportunities at the same time. Opportunities for environmental savvy citizens, with the focus on a more regional and sustainable agriculture, also as a preventive measure for civil unrest in times of currency crisis and increasing unemployment numbers.

"Our population and our use of the finite resources of planet Earth are growing exponentially, along with our technical ability to change the environment for good or ill."

– Stephen Hawking

18

INFORMATION EQUALITY

All information – with the exception of illegal or extremist materials or data that violates individual human- or privacy rights – should be publicly available for a society to discuss and evaluate from a scientific perspective. While some sort of filtering in technological gray areas will always be required for reasons of national security, a basic and unfiltered access to digital information in general should be a fundamental right. As previously already discussed as 'right to internet access' or 'right to broadband' and already recognized under the right to exercise freedom of expression by many countries, internet access can already be seen as an integral part of social-cultural participation.

Especially since many previously paper-based tasks as employment applications are bound to the internet already, the assumption should always be the case of an unemployed citizen without any funds, trying to find a job as a justification for a basic public internet access to governmental- or unemployment services. Together with additional digital governmental paperless services, such a public access could further act as the cornerstone for a large cost reduction in the administrative sector.

"Knowledge is power. Information is liberating. Education is the premise of progress, in every society, in every family."

– Kofi Annan

PART IV

A SMART TAXATION MODEL

19

SO HOW IS REVENUE GENERATED?

Considering all the obviously social aspects in this book, someone might be quick at asking where in the world all the subsidize is taken from. The solution lies – unlike assumed – not in the raise of any taxes, but in the German translation of the word "taxation" but in it's pristine sense. To "steer" / "govern" / "navigate".

Taxes should always and only be taken from products, services or businesses according to their positive or negative impact on a society.

By an increased taxation of what's bad in a society, but only so slightly that it is not too much restrictive for consumers, negative habits can be opposed with healthier or more educative products and services in the long-term.

A quit powerful approach in contrast to a taxation-model that mostly decides between consumer products, groceries, alcohol, tobacco and gasoline as categories. Instead, a shift towards a more unified taxation system that subjects as much positive and negative aspects of our daily life's as possible to either taxation or subsidize – even if only by a few cents to be not overly restrictive.

In general, a broad selection of rating standards for a more precise taxation of goods and services according their health-, social- and environmental impact. Rating criteria that would obviously have to be defined by a well selected authority of educated citizens as the best possible representation of common sense. Preferably, public or semi-public employed citizens who work in social related fields to avoid possible influence of private interests.

The following unified taxation model resembles more of a first draft that could lead to such a broader accepted and transparent form of taxation later on. But once applied, it could drastically change consumer decisions without any additional restrictions or increased taxation.

20

A UNIFIED TAXATION MODEL

So how does it work?

From an objective point of view, there are basically 5 criteria that define all aspects of our society that are mostly negatively influenced by corporate interests and lobbying today, creating an endless self-reasoning system of unnecessary problems and long-term effects.

And due to the interconnection of these 5 main categories, any rating of related goods and services automatically solves many even remotely related problems at once, and not just the obvious ones.

Our environment affects our health and the quality of our nutrition. An unhealthy nutrition affects our health and obviously leads to rising healthcare costs. Our health itself affects the economy and our families well being, including overseen social related side effects such as less flexibility to spent time for our kids education in the case of illnesses in a family.

The same way violent media, alcohol, tobacco and drugs are a main cause for all kinds of health and family-related problems and a less productive society, every small influence to one of these main categories affects at least one of the other categories too. An interconnected circle of life.

5 criteria that define all major aspects of society:

Health – *Is it beneficial for health?*

Family – *Is it socially beneficial?*

Education – *Is it educative?*

Economy – *Is it efficient and ethical labored?*

Environment – *Is it environmentally friendly?*

The idea of a positive or negative taxation of all types of products or services – even if only by a few cents – could be seen as dictatorship on customer decisions, yet in fact, such a model based on a democratic rating by a predefined group of applicable and educated citizens (To be specific, teachers or nurses, as an example of health aware citizens who work in the public sector with human relations) could simply shift the tax revenue directly to root causes for most of all these day-to-day problems. From Industry and lobbying influenced goods and services, as the root cause for pretty much all social or health-related problems to environmental issues, to unhealthy manufacturing or laboring standards, to the educational quality of television and media. With the possibility of a full tax-subsidize to goods or services that have a positive effect, such as sustainable or fair-trade grown foods or health-, fitness or sport related activities.

As a first cornerstone, enforcement of a healthier nutrition is not only important from an ethical perspective, but simultaneously also removes the weight and burden of an ever increasingly struggling healthcare system. Healthy eating and a health-aware lifestyle as a cost-saving approach and prevention of cardiovascular diseases and cancer related costs in a population. Likewise, a population educated due to more restrictive food labeling and subsidize programs for any type of sport activity might also become more intelligent and health-aware, and therefor more efficient as a side effect.

As a long-term goal, this approach could easily have a large impact of the overall health, intelligence and efficiency of a society, consequently leading to more innovation and higher productivity.

Contrary to the current desire of the food industry to sell the most processed sugars, high-fructose corn products and white flour, an increased taxation of questionable food additives, added sugars but also cholesterol, trans-fats and saturated fats, additional to the existing health-aware taxation models of alcohol and tobacco. But in a unified way, with alcohol or tobacco as subcategories under the category 'Health Tax' - even though with their different percentage of taxation – and not as their own taxation categories.

In other words; a general – but social- and health aware defined – regulation of a populations dietary decisions from the tax-subsidize for healthy food products to the maximum amount of taxation for alcohol and tobacco. But also non-organic grown foods and sugary beverages could receive a higher taxation of only a few cents as a subsidize for organic agriculture and unquestionable healthier alternatives like bottled water. Even further, knowing about the useless carbon footprint of bottled water, an even higher oversight of the quality of tap-water and a subsidize program for household carbonizers to stimulate the consumption of tap-water instead of bottled beverages could be an additional option.

"Physical fitness is not only one of the most important keys to a healthy body, it is the basis of dynamic and creative intellectual activity."

– John F. Kennedy

Example of smart-taxation oriented recipe

```
******** GROCERY STORE ********
────────────────────────────────────────
PIZZA                 10 %         1.99
FRENCH FRIES          10 %         2.99
SOFT DRINK            25 %         0.99
ICE CREAM             25 %         2.99
WHISKEY               30 %         8.99
MOTOR OIL             30 %         7.99

CHICKEN BREAST       -10 %         6.99
CARROTS              -10 %         2.99
OATMEAL              -10 %         1.99
KIDS BOOK            -10 %         6.99
SCHOOL BOOK          -10 %         7.99
OFFICE PLANNER       -10 %        24.99

+++ SUBTOTAL                      77.88
+++ TAX                            3.79
      + HEALTH        5.39
      + FAMILY       -0.70
      + EDUCATION    -0.80
      + ECONOMY      -2.50
      + ENVIRONMENT   2.40
+++ TOTAL                         81.67
```

Example of smart-taxation oriented nutrition

label

Nutrition Facts

10 servings per container

200 Calories (per 55g)

% DV*

10%	**Total Protein**	**5g**
10%	**Total Fat**	**7g**
10%	Saturated Fat	2g
0%	Transfat	0g
0%	Cholesterol	0mg
10%	**Total Carbs**	**23g**
10%	Dietary Fiber	2g
10%	Sugars	9g

~%	**Minerals, Vitamins**	
10%	Sodium	600mg
10%	Vitamin D	1mcg
10%	Calcium	100mg
10%	Iron	2mg
10%	Potassium	470mg

0% Health Tax +++

☑ Organic & Low Waste ♻

* Footnote on Daily Values (DV) and
calories reference to be inserted here.

Nutrition Facts

10 servings per container

370 Calories (per 55g)

% DV*

1%	**Total Protein**	**1g**
25%	**Total Fat**	**18g**
90%	Saturated Fat !	18g
0%	Transfat	0g
0%	Cholesterol	0mg
15%	**Total Carbs**	**35g**
0%	Dietary Fiber	0g
48%	Sugars	35g

~%	**Minerals, Vitamins**	
20%	Sodium	1200mg
0%	Vitamin D	0mcg
1%	Calcium	10mg
0%	Iron	0mg
1%	Potassium	5mg

15% Health Tax +++

* Footnote on Daily Values (DV) and calories
reference to be inserted here.

21

TAXATION OF AUTOMATION

Since the beginning of our industrial era, automation lead not only to an increased productivity, but also allowed for the first time an availability of products that were once to costly to manufacture for the broader public, with the automobile as the best example. However, in just the recent years, automation technology also continuously removed jobs that once provided work for large parts of our society and were previously unaffected by it. Not only in the manufacturing industry, but increasingly in fields that were previously exempt from automation but now became redundant only due to changes in the way we access information or **services**.

With many jobs that always used to be a part in our society like the ticket accountant or travel agency accountant that are being shifted to the internet and mobile apps as one example, the future of accounting- and service-jobs outside the gastronomy-, retail-, or health and beauty-related services industry is hard to predict.

Additional to that, with automation as an indelible part in our modern industry, a social-security fee for machine automated laboring tasks would be impossible to enforce **retrospectively**, but still be applied to new automation and digitization of accounting services today. A model that considers certain types of digital services to a small amount of additional taxation could act as a buffer for welfare cost related revenue required in the meantime.

However, even with the increasing amount of automation in our society that ultimately leads to a higher efficiency, there will always be jobs in the educational, medicare and social sector. In a futuristic economy, pretty much everyone should work in either science, education or the health- and elderly care sector, without all the overhead of today's public sector. It's hard to predict if there will ever be a point when human industrial labor will fully be automated in the first world out of ethical reasons, considering that any form of labor in less developed countries – even if intellectual – might always remain cheaper. Instead, it should be common sense that – and despite all the tempting economical benefits of cheap imports – imported products have at least to be manufactured according to the same labor rights of our first world and with the maximum amount of oversight to enforce these rights.

In the same way we would not wish for our own children nor even the neighbors kids to be raised up in the in the trashcan in front of our houses, we should not blend out the situation in developing countries only because we benefit from it so conveniently.

A taxation model that subjects imports of products that are 'fair trade' to a slightly lower taxation then other imports would be an obvious solution that applies to ethical labor in other countries.

But additionally, taxation that subjects automation in general would also be an often referred concept to counterweight the societal impact of advanced automation. A precise taxation model that differs between primitive automation replacing inhuman working tasks as beneficial from a social aspect, and advanced automation that removes ethical industrial jobs to receive additional taxation.

...

"In the twenty-first century, the robot will take the place which slave labor occupied in ancient civilization."

– Nikola Tesla

22

TAXATION OF GOODS BY THEIR EFFICIENCY FOOTPRINT

Considering not only the total carbon and water footprint of products, but also the weight-based carbon efficiency of materials itself depending on its life-cycle and use case. In the automotive sector it would result in the enforcement of an increasing use of aluminum based alloys and environmental friendly lightweight composites and fabrics and a decreasing use of heavy steel parts, heavy rubbers and leathers. A general direction towards more easily recyclable plastics and aluminum parts, but also towards a preference of lightweight product designs that save energy in consideration of their total carbon footprint over lifetime.

Another significant point could be a new weight-rating for consumer products in general, subject to the 'Environment' category of the unified taxation model, knowing that weight not only adds to the carbon footprint over the lifecycle of a product, but additionally to the energy required in the recycling process. Packaging would be an obvious example that is already restricted and became even more efficient by the desire of vendors to ship as much goods per cargo. Other day to day items, such as household tools – with the exception of professional tools – are often not subject to an efficient design.

23

ETHICAL GOODS & SERVICES

Non-educative, obsessive violent or by times extremist content accounts for a large part of media in our digital life's. The same way, products or goods that are unhealthy have a negative impact on a society and are subject to a rating under health taxation, all type of media that is questionable from an educational perspective should at least receive a mildly higher taxation than content that is unquestionable ethical or educative.

A taxation and subsidization of related goods and services by a beneficial factor rating by an authority of qualified and educated citizens could counterweight content with the most negative effects, such as obsessive violent or inhuman media that have a negative influence on a younger generation exposed to it.

As a representation of common sense, all citizens above the age of 30, who work in social beneficial branches such as as education, healthcare and public services and who preferably have kids would be most applicable to categorize individual media according to their social- or educative value. Additionally, every responsible mother would also automatically be best suited to up- and down vote certain types of fast-food, groceries or individual types of kids toys via a simple online report form.

Such a broad rating model for day-to-day consumer goods could not only to eradicate many social- or health related problems, but also force larger brands to rethink the educational- or nutritional value of their well known traditional products; Increasingly leading to a competition for the most educative or nutritious products within likely just a few weeks after implementation.

...

4

AUTOMATED INCOME & REVENUE TAXATION

There are many possible technical approaches, but a bank-account centered taxation system detailed in the next chapter could eradicate pretty much all the current administrative overhead and redundant work in tax collecting agencies. Debatable might be the social aspect of an automatic negative income tax for those who fall under specific amount of income, but in combination with the already existing social security identifiers it would make the exact amount of tax calculated not only paper-less, but also transparent and fair for everyone. At the same time, increasingly shifting resources of taxation accounting to the oversight of smarter regulations in the financial-, food-, pharmaceutical-, and medical industry. In a time, were we already have these large databases with unique identifiers, knowing everything about everyone of us for surveillance reasons, it would only be smart to use the exact same data to save on the administrative overhead of tax-collection. Obviously, with the highest respect for privacy rights and individual freedoms, but statistically to optimize tax-collection of previous gray areas, loopholes and offshore havens.

The following model resembles more of a first idea to that.

THE CITIZENS CREDIT CARD

The same way the passport already acts as a public ID card that is representing the fictitious corporation of citizenship we have since birth, the citizens credit card resembles a fictitious bank account that is created at birth to be used for all governmental financial transactions received or send by a citizen during lifetime.

Before the age of 18, the cards transactions are linked to the card of a corresponding parent. From welfare or child support to later income taxation, the citizens credit card eradicates the administrative overhead of many governmental services by an automated age- and taxation based algorithm. In that respect, all private bank accounts and liabilities a citizen possesses since birth are directly linked to it, with all categories of taxation already applied accordingly. From Income taxation, healthcare fees, vehicle taxation, internet, rental, housing and power utility. A transparency that might be rejected by many citizens, but knowing that these datasets are already collected in either way, it would simply educate a broader public about the transparency of their possessions or service contracts.

In detail: the citizens credit card replaces the citizens social security ID, public healthcare ID and taxation ID with one unified identifier. Instead of filing a tax report, it would be simply required by law to have all private bank accounts connected to it, and all taxation and benefits are calculated based on the corresponding categories, subject to a different rating for certain categories.

In the case of taxation-payments or legal fines, the charge could be on hold until the citizen authorities it via an online form to be charged from a linked private bank account, comparable to the current situation of tax collection when taxation charges are 'due' until paid. Especially to avoid an additional burden to the already struggling bottom- and middle class.

In the case of welfare; rent, gas and power utility are automatically paid to the corresponding providers to prevent any misuse of governmental support.

In the case of child support, the amount of a teenagers daily spending amount could be directly available on the card itself, further preventing misuse child support by irresponsible parents.

With such a model, most of the dispensable bureaucratic jobs in the previous paper-based administrations could be shifted to the increased and more important oversight of smarter regulations in the financial-, food-, pharmaceutical or medical industry. But also to oversight in public areas, such as environmental or wildlife protection that lack funds today.

Instead of Taxation accounting, healthcare-insurance accounting and social service accounting in the public sector that become redundant to a degree, there will further also be more resources for human relations and individual help. Resources to focus on the important social aspects of life, such as education at first and foremost but also the administration of public sport activities and programs to enforce a more health aware lifestyle.

First revision. To be continued..

AFTERWORDS

I finished and uploaded most of this content in august 2014, but due to a specific reason I was withheld from finishing the remaining chapters for almost 7 months. Realizing that I became increasingly less capable to even write a single sentence, I considered the idea of closing this already very short book with quite a few empty pages. But I decided against it when I regained some of my abilities. The hardcover version will use a slightly thicker white paper to be a full pocket-book. Because it is impossible to give more than 100%, this first revision simply closes way earlier than intended.

MY LIFE

SO CLOSE TO NEVER HAPPEN

There are many scriptures in history based on true events and unprecedented in their tragedy. From the holy scriptures, to some of Shakespeare's works or Charles Dickens 'Oliver Twist'. And there are so many great novels of our modern time that define social drama in the same way, unsurpassed in the detailing of complicated family-ties. Even until today.

As mostly everyone, I grew up with many of the same classic literature or common children's books. Always with the warm sense of security my two lovely parents raised me up with, certain my life wouldn't be anything out of the ordinary and free from any tragedies or drama.

And I kept this sense of security until my late twenties, and even then – with lost friendships and abrupt health problems – I always had my gifted childhood and early youth to look back and rely on. Everything seemed to be so perfect.

And back then, it really had been all so perfect. But writing these first words now frightens me to be unable to cope with the rest of my actual life's story that points back so far to this time. And even more because I came to know about the full outreach of it only about a year ago. But there is no one else but me who committed enough to be allowed to write it down. Apart from legal materials that are already in save hands, it just took me more than this whole year to recover and regain enough memories to understand. Memories to a chain of events, in my unique case likely unprecedented in the history of mostly any modern society, yet still favorable enough I was given the chance to become aware of them to write it down. At least to this moment.

...

I gave this world to you.

– Florian

First Draft Published, August 15, 2014

SBN-13: 978-1508821168